Girlfriends

One Hundred Original Quotations to Inspire You to Keep Flying

Karen Danage

Girlfriends

One Hundred Original Quotations to Inspire You to Keep Flying

Karen Danage

FROM:

Secret Friend ♡

TO:

Katie

A Note of Thanks

I want to thank my husband of twenty-eight years, Robert, and Deylon and Kayla, my son and daughter. They have supported me throughout my journey.

In addition, I wish to thank my mentors at the Small Business Development Center in Dallas, Texas, and Knowledge for Success in Fort Worth, Texas. They stayed by my side for more than seven years and provided me with valuable information and guidance.

Lastly, I want to thank Ms. Lillian Stokes, my sixth-grade teacher, who discovered my passion for writing and told me, "Karen, never stop writing."

Introduction

About two years ago, while frying chicken for our traditional Sunday dinner, I fainted. I came to and stumbled to the bathroom, where I passed out again. Upon coming to again, I was shocked to find blood all over my bathroom. My children were upstairs, unaware of what had happened. I yelled for help, and they rushed me to the emergency room. The ER doctor discovered a tumor in my stomach. As a result, I was advised to have surgery immediately and a biopsy to ensure the tumor was not malignant. I was at a loss for words; I couldn't believe this was happening. The doctor informed me in a very matter-of-fact manner that this incident could have been fatal.

As I lay in my hospital bed, recovering from surgery and waiting for the biopsy results, I began to think about my life. I believe that when a person is faced with death, what really matters is quickly revealed. I immediately thought about two things: my family and my thirty-year journey as a writer. My passion for writing was discovered by my sixth-grade teacher, Ms. Lillian Stokes, at Memphis Campus School in Memphis, Tennessee. I captured her attention with a short story titled, "The Little Green Man," as well as many other poems and short stories. She believed in me and told me, "Karen, never stop writing." I will always remember her words.

I made a vow to complete the books I had started writing, and I recommitted myself to my product line, Heartration Products, which I launched in March 2010.

When I learned that the biopsy results were negative, I waited for everyone to leave the room. Then I began to cry. I thanked God for sparing my life, and I knew without a doubt that I was still alive for a reason. Later that evening, I picked up a pad and pen—which I always have with me—and began to write a poem called "Girlfriends." I decided this would be the title of my first book.

As women, we are all on a journey, ultimately trying to fulfill our destiny. Each of us has a story to tell. I believe it is my destiny and time to inspire others through my words. I hope your heart is touched and, most importantly, that you become inspired to live the life you are destined to live. I made the decision to stop just flapping my wings and instead to fly because, as I experienced through my illness, I don't know when my last day will be.

As you read *Girlfriends*, I hope you reimagine your own journey.

Girlfriends

We are the color of midnight, brown, yellow, white, and caramel. Our faces don't always show the scars life left during the battles; we have endured. We are all on a journey, trying to reach our destinations and fulfill our destinies. Look into the sky, and you will see millions of butterflies flying with astonishing grace and dignity. Some are missing a wing; some have had to replace their wings; some have patched up their wings; and many have holes in their wings. If you look closely, you will see some carrying others on their backs because they are friends. Let's not take for granted our girlfriends; instead, let's encourage them, respect them, protect them, uphold them, and, most importantly, help them fly.

From my heart to yours—keep flying.

Karen

Contents

Adversity 1

To dine with success, you must be willing to cook in adversity's kitchen.

Success is a journey, and adversity is often the main ingredient in its recipe. Remember: some of the most successful ideas are not cooked in success's kitchen, but adversity's.

Adversity 2

Adversity is always willing to help you find the exit signs.

Do you ever feel like quitting? You can't give up on your dreams. You must learn how to fight like a gladiator. The next time adversity whispers in your ear, "Quit," tell it to beat it.

Adversity 3

Attaining the honey in life is a great accomplishment; but not being stung by the bees of adversity is the real challenge.

Can you endure the stings of adversity? Adversity builds your immune system and enables you to withstand adversity's stings and even thrive when confronted with them.

Adversity 4

The winds of adversity are often used to blow you into your purpose.

Losing a loved one, becoming ill, being fired from a dream job, or facing any setback may seem to be the end of the road. However, sometimes we must lose in order to gain. It is during tough times that we are forced to reinvent ourselves, and often, to our surprise, we discover that greatness lies within.

Adversity 5

Don't allow adversity's tornadoes to destroy your dreams.

A tornado can destroy all that's in its path, leaving fragments of what used to be. Adversity can also destroy dreams just like a tornado. Have you experienced adversity? Perhaps it was not getting a promotion, a foreclosure, or a bad business decision. Recovery is possible. It may take time and patience, but your dreams are worth rebuilding.

Believe 6

In order to achieve, you must first believe.

If you believe it is attainable, you can accomplish it. There is a great teacher, chef, mother, wife, inspirational speaker, or lawyer inside of you, waiting to be unleashed. However, it is during the process of becoming that we often give up. Begin seeing yourself as a work in progress—not as a finished product.

Believe 7

Rejection will not kill your dreams. Not believing in them will.

How many times have you heard "no"; how many companies have told you that they are not hiring; how many bank loans have you been denied? Rejection is like being bitten by fire ants; it hurts. Believing is like oxygen. It will ease the pain and stop your dreams from dying.

Believe 8

Women who believe they can do the impossible will not run from giants. They will slay them.

Being the tallest, strongest, and best looking doesn't guarantee that you will conquer the giants in your life. The individual everyone underestimates is often the giant slayer because that person believes. Remember, it only takes one stone to slay the giants in your life.

Believe 9

The stars may seem out of your reach, but you can catch them if you believe.

Your dreams are achievable. But you won't accomplish them by gazing out of your window into the sky. You will attain them by reaching every day until you catch them. They are closer than you think.

Believe 10

Don't allow your inadequacies to lock you up. Believing always has a spare cuff key.

Millions of people are doing hard time because they have allowed their inadequacies to give them a life sentence. It is time to break free. You must believe that your future is still bright—despite your imperfections.

Denial 11

If denial is allowed to dwell, truth can't become an occupant.

When I made the decision to face the denial that existed in my life and accept truth, I began to seek solutions and the restoration process began. The areas of denial that once held me captive now represent areas of strength, growth, and stability.

Denial 12

Denial will make you believe you are walking on a cloud when you are sinking in quicksand.

What or who is pulling you into the quicksand? Before you sink so deep that you can't resurface, you must face the reality of whatever is making you sink. Pretending that all is well is not going to change the circumstances. Face your problem before it is too late.

Denial 13

Denying your dreams means living a life shackled by limitations.

The inventors of liquid paper, disposal diapers, windshield wipers, and cosmetics removed the shackles of limitations by allowing themselves to dream. They turned their dreams into realities by creating products that improved the quality of their lives and the lives of many others.

Denial 14

Denying who you are is a dangerous game to play because you could lose yourself forever.

Sometimes, you change who you are to accommodate others out of the fear of losing them. Then one day you don't recognize yourself anymore. Like a little girl looking for her lost doll, you begin to search for *you*. You are worth holding on to. Never compromise yourself to please others.

Denial 15

At twenty, I settled into my box.
At thirty, I remolded my box.
At forty, I realized I was in denial about living in a box.
At fifty, I demolished the box.

How many times have you been put into a box—boxed in because of your gender, income, or ethnicity? At times, the box seems like a safe place, but be careful not to become "boxed in." We are all at different stages and places on the journey, but one place we never want to become trapped in is the box. Who or what is boxing you in?

Destiny 16

Why do you keep borrowing your girlfriend's shoes? There is a custom pair made for you to walk into your destiny.

Can you imagine wearing hiking boots when you should be wearing tennis shoes? Your girlfriend's journey is not yours. Make sure you are wearing your own shoes. Return the borrowed shoes and start wearing your own so you can fulfill your unique purpose.

Destiny 17

I know you are tired, but the rest stop was not designed for you to stay there. It is time to get back on the road. You have not reached your destination.

I love road trips. The rest stops give me an opportunity to get a cold drink and stretch my legs. But rest stops were not built for us to stay there. They provide us with a place to take a short break. Don't allow the rest stop to become a detour. Take a deep breath and open your car door; it is time to get back on the road.

Destiny 18

Close your eyes. See yourself dancing with destiny to the lyrics of unlimited possibilities. You can make the decision each day to live your life in an extraordinary way.

Who is your dance partner? Is it doubt, fear, unbelief, regret, or procrastination? Destiny is asking you to be its dance partner. Don't say no. This is the most important dance of your life.

Destiny 19

An optimist clearly sees her destiny—even in the fog.

I challenge you to become an optimist. When you feel optimism, you can see your destiny during the blizzards, thunderstorms, and, yes, in the fog. The lesson is this: you must always have a clear vision of your destiny even when you can't see it.

Destiny 20

Don't look at the designer shoes of successful women. Look at the soles of their feet. They received the blisters from walking miles to reach their destiny.

How far are you willing to walk? Often, we admire the glitz and glam of successful women. But if we learn how they conducted their journey and mastered their pain, we too can achieve success.

Dream 21

Risk looking crazy to others to accomplish your dreams.

Your dreams may be so big they appear to others to be impossible to accomplish. They think you are crazy. Don't take it personally; instead, keep working on your dreams until they become realities. Remember, some of the most famous innovators were laughed at and often misunderstood. However, when their dreams became a reality, the laughs turned in to cheers, applause, and compliments.

Dream 22

There is no expiration date on your dreams.

Imagine thousands of neatly stacked boxes, each containing our lost dreams, sitting in the lost and found department. They were dropped there one by one, and we never returned to look for them. It is never too late. Claim your dreams today. They have been waiting for you.

Dream 23

Your dreams are like a garden. They must be fertilized to grow.

Perhaps the reason your dreams have not grown is due to bad fertilizer. You must nurture your dreams and protect them against disease and toxicity in the form of negative people or words of discouragement such as, "You can't; your dreams are too big." It is time to fertilize those dreams with love and care.

Dream 24

Don't treat your dreams like a partially constructed building or they could be demolished.

Is there a project, a dream, or a goal you started working on, and one day you decided to take a thirty-minute break that turned into a five-year break? You were excited and had so much passion, but you began to get tired. If you woke up this morning, there is still time to finish. Don't live a half-constructed life. Make a decision today and finish the project—no matter what.

ᗪream 25

Doubting you can accomplish your dreams is like living in a house with termites. Your dreams will be destroyed one by one.

Doubting is powerful. It can erode your passion and energy. You must focus and guard your dreams like rare gems. Think of all the inventions, screenplays, and business concepts that have made millions of dollars. Each one of them began as a dream.

Encouragement 26

Encouragement is like an antibiotic. It can heal a broken heart.

When you are discouraged, your heart can feel as if it has been broken. You face so many challenges in life. They can begin to pull at your heart strings. Many events in my life have made me feel as though my heart was broken. Sometimes it takes years for your heart to heal, depending on how badly you were wounded. You must feed your heart encouragement, such as reading inspirational quotes or scriptures or listening to good sermons. Try to begin your day with words of encouragement.

Engouragement 27

Encouragement is like a cashmere sweater. It will keep you warm when you are in life's snowstorm.

The seasons of life include snow, sunshine, rain, and, unfortunately, a lot of stormy weather. The question is this: what do you do when you find yourself cold and alone? You should put on encouragement's cashmere sweater; it will keep you warm during the snowstorm.

Encouragement 28

Discouragement is like being a mountain lion without teeth—defenseless. But don't worry; encouragement has dentures. It can fight back.

Discouragement can make you vulnerable and weak. You can lose your ability to fight back. Life is going to place each of us in some difficult situations, because that is life. You can survive by staying encouraged, no matter what the circumstances are.

Encouragement 29

You are on the ropes, and it looks like you have lost the fight. But this is a tag-team match, and encouragement is stepping into the ring.

Are there days when you feel as though you have been in the boxing ring with discouragement? I experienced this when I was recovering from surgery. It seemed as if I would never recover from the pain that engulfed my body. I focused on getting better and on the fact that I was still alive. I was in the ring with discouragement, but I was determined to win the fight. Whatever you are facing today, don't let discouragement keep you on the ropes. Fight back with a left hook.

Encouragement 30

You have broken down on life's highway. Don't panic. Encouragement runs a twenty-four-hour towing service.

You can't drive another mile. You are stranded on the highway because you don't see a way out of the daily grind. You must learn how to repair your soul and refuel your engine before you run out of gas. Often, the demands life places on you keep you so busy that you ignore the warning signs. Don't allow your engine to overheat. Get your tune-ups at encouragement's garage.

Faith 31

Faith is like an insect repellent: it keeps defeat from biting you.

Faith enables you to smile even though you cried yourself to sleep last night. It enables you to go on the twenty-fifth job interview despite having to ride the bus because you don't own a car. Faith enables you to plan on buying a home, firmly stating, "One day, I will be a homeowner." Faith keeps defeat from biting you because you believe deep down inside that you will make it.

Faith 32

Faith will enable you to transform from ordinary to extraordinary.

Don't make the mistake of comparing yourself with others. Your extraordinary may not look like your girl-friend's. You should perform at your own level. I know some extraordinary bakers, teachers, doctors, hair stylists, and ministers. They have transformed their ordinary into extraordinary by being the very best at what they do.

Faith 33

It's not your super-sized wings that will enable you to fly through the storms. It is your faith.

If you change your perspective and see the storms as opportunities to increase your faith, those events that could have destroyed you will become assets instead of liabilities.

Faith 34

Faith produces diamonds; procrastination produces rocks.

Someday I will go back to school, write a book, lose weight, love again, change occupations—and the list goes on. Don't allow procrastination to steal your dreams and don't "someday" your life away. Begin with tiny steps toward your goals. Your faith will allow you to complete the project. So don't delay. Dump the rocks and find the *diamonds!*

Faith 35

Your faith is like a car engine. It has to be turned on.

Can you imagine getting a call from your girlfriend, announcing that she is taking you on a shopping spree? Wow—every girl's dream! You wait for an hour, but she doesn't arrive. You call her, only to learn that she is sitting in her driveway because she was too worried (about any number of things) to turn the engine on. It is not enough to talk about faith or hear the best inspirational sermons on faith. You must turn your faith on, or you may find yourself just sitting there.

Fly 36

Flapping your wings is not the tragedy—never flying is.

One of my biggest fears was never publishing. I had thoughts of a stranger discovering my manuscripts at a garage sale, hidden in a suitcase. I made a decision that I would publish and fulfill my dreams. I decided it was time to stop flapping my wings—and start flying.

Fly 37

You will never soar in your life if you keep meeting the chickens for coffee.

I love coffee shops and the cozy atmosphere they offer. I believe those we choose to meet for coffee can have an impact on our lives. The conversations you engage in may be keeping you from accomplishing your dreams. Who we associate with is a reflection of who we are. The next time you meet your girlfriends for coffee, ask them are they eagles or chickens. You may be surprised to find out whom you have been meeting for coffee.

Fly 38

You will never grow your wings meeting the alley cats for dinner. Those cats have no interest in ever learning to fly.

It may sound arrogant, but if you intend on soaring beyond where you are, the first step is to lose the losers. Too many people are afraid to leave the pack. It is easy to blend into a group, but it takes guts to stand alone.

Fly 39

Choose to fly above others—not by striving to be equal but by excelling.

Each of us is unique. Because of this, some will fly higher than others, depending on their mission in life. However, each of us should be flying at our own altitude instead of trying to fly with the flock. Be the very best at what you do, and you will excel.

Girlfriends 40

Sometimes life surprises us with unexpected gifts throughout the journey.
Your friendship is one of them.
We've been through a lot together.
Yet we are still laughing,
Still climbing mountains,
Still achieving our dreams, and
Still flying, despite the holes in our wings.

Real friendship is a gift money can't buy. Time changes our perceptions as we take inventory of our relationships; we come to realize they are more than socializing on a girls' night out. Friendship requires resilience and commitment. Take the time today to let your girlfriends know how much they mean to you.

Girlfriends 41

When the storms of life blow, I will cover you like a cloak. Don't despair, for life sometimes is unfair. Wipe your tears and hold your head up high, and don't walk but fly! At the end of life's journey, you will find your girlfriends by your side.

There is no better feeling than to experience true friendship. To know you can depend on someone other than yourself is more precious than gold. We must be careful not to judge others' dependence or assume that we are self-reliant. Life has a way of reminding each of us through its circumstances how vulnerable we are as human beings. Decide today to become a cloak.

Girlfriends 42

You should treat some friends like bunions on your feet—cut them off.

Bunions are very painful and sometimes they must be surgically removed. Some friends in your life may be causing you pain and discomfort. It is not easy sometimes to let them go, but if certain friends leave you in a constant state of pain, it may be time to cut them off.

Girlfriends 43

Like superheroes, we come to one another's rescue in times of trouble. That is why I keep my pink cape nearby—in case you call.

We all need friends who will be there when we send out an SOS. Life can land some hard punches that sometimes require someone to help you get up from the floor.

Girlfriends 44

Loyalty wears steel-toe boots instead of stilettos. She is ready to walk the distance with you.

Loyal friends are an endangered species. They are very hard to find. Loyalty will stand with you in the rain without an umbrella; loyalty will stick by your side if you have three hundred dollars or a million; loyalty will not leave you stranded on the highway but gives you a ride; loyalty hands you a tissue to wipe your tears and doesn't ask questions. Are you wearing steel-toe boots or stilettos?

God's Love 45

God never takes a vacation or uses a sick day.

I believe God and his angels were looking over me on Sunday, December 18, 2011, when I fainted twice from a tumor in my stomach. That day could have been my last. God is on his job 24/7. He is always watching over us, and, unlike humans, he never gets tired or needs eight hours of sleep.

God's Love 46

God hides the blueprint of our life to keep us from erasing the bumpy roads.

If we knew all of the trials and hard times we were going to face, most of us would avoid them. But then, how would we ever become stronger? God locks the blueprints in a vault so that we can't alter them. We must learn how to trust God. He is in the control center of our lives and is a master strategist. He will help us navigate our way through the difficult times, helping us to grow stronger in the process.

God's Love 47

God's love is as sweet as apple pie—but without the calories. Have another serving; it won't increase your waistline.

God's love is as sweet as your most favorite dessert, but it's calorie-free. Sometimes we will require his love to get us through those difficult situations when our backs are against the wall. He made promises to love each of us no matter what. That is a powerful commitment. Have a serving today.

God's Love 48

God can't touch your heart because you have covered it with Scotchgard.

With each painful event or disappointment, you begin to use Scotchgard on your heart. Then one day before you know it, your heart is fully covered, and God has no way of touching it. I have been there, with my hand balled tightly, stating, "I will never be hurt again." However, I have learned to trust God. When you trust him, he begins to mend the holes in your heart. If you have covered your heart with Scotchgard, it may be time to remove it.

God's Love 49

God sometimes has to maneuver through the manure in our life to find us.

I am glad God doesn't mind manure. He is willing to get his hands dirty, reaching into the sewers to find us if he has to. It doesn't matter how many times we have messed up. He doesn't keep a record of our mistakes. He runs the best janitorial service and is ready with a mop, bucket, and bleach to wipe away our messes.

God's Love 50

You don't have to use the layaway to purchase a new beginning. God will pay for it in full.

You don't have to make monthly payments on a new beginning because you are desperate for a fresh start. God is ready to pay for it in full. Some of us entered the world with the odds against us, and some of us placed ourselves in a dark place. It doesn't matter whether you are rich, poor, black, brown, yellow, or white—he loves everyone the same. If you need a new start, call heaven today; your new beginning will be express mailed free of charge.

Integrity 51

Let integrity be your flashlight when compromise turns off the lights.

Every year, we read and hear about the scandals. They range from defrauding millions of dollars or athletes compromising themself by taking medications that give them an unfair advantage over their opponents. They need to be the best or the richest at any cost, but, in the end, they lose. Like a run in your pantyhose, the circumstances around lies begin to unravel, and the holes in the story can't be fixed fast enough. A small detail may be missed, or someone trusted during the scheme reports it into the authorities. Integrity keeps us from the pitfalls that can lead to prison, demotions, damaged relationships, and sometimes a lifetime of embarrassment. The next time you are tempted to compromise, pull out your flashlight.

Integrity 52

A contractual agreement will stand tall when integrity gets amnesia.

She seemed so nice, you thought. However, you should have used a contract. It is a lesson some of us learned the hard way. I have been burned when I didn't stick to the rules of engagement when doing business. People can be very good actors. As a result, I was convinced a contract was not needed until it was too late. The lesson? Business is business. Emotions won't protect you in court, but a contract will.

Integrity 53

Some friends will steal your money, designer shoes, boyfriend, or husband and then help you look for them.

Sometimes the people closest to us will take our "stuff." Has your best friend ever hurt you? Why did it hurt so badly? Because your guard was down, and the gates to your heart were wide open. Friendship is a responsibility; it takes integrity to ensure that you are treating others as you would like to be treated. Embrace your life and don't allow the green-eyed monster called envy to sabotage your relationships or cause you to take what is not yours.

Integrity 54

Your charm and charisma will get you to the top of the mountain, but your integrity will keep you there.

Because of reality television, many people have become success stories overnight. The CEO goes undercover, and the employees have no idea who the CEO really is. He or she wants to find out how to improve the company and to find out which employees have integrity. When the CEO is revealed, of course the employees are shocked, but the best part of the show is when the CEO rewards those employees with integrity. We should try to live in this manner and act as if our life were being filmed.

Integrity 55

Integrity is willing to eat mud pie so that it can eventually enjoy the pound cake.

It sounds noble to say that you have integrity, but you may lose some friends and even experience setbacks because of your decisions. But in the end, you will not regret doing what's right. If you are eating mud pies, remember that there is a pound cake being baked just for you in integrity's bakery.

Issues 56

It's time to send your issues to the retirement community. They have worked long enough.

Allowing your toxic issues to live year after year can begin to take a toll on you emotionally, mentally, spirituality, and physically. When you address them and let them retire, you are going to feel like a new person.

Issues 57

You can't take off the runway due to the excess baggage. It is time to dump the issues.

Are you carrying extra baggage—carrying everyone else's problems and burdens, including your own? Consequently, you are weighed down and can't take off the runway. Be careful not to miss your opportunities. It should be a wake-up call when the same individuals you helped are now flying, and you are still sitting on the runway. Today is the day to dump the excess baggage. The air traffic control center just called for your plane to take off. Don't miss taking flight this time.

Issues 58

Issues are like roaches. They run when the lights are turned on.

Several years ago, I attended a women's conference with a close friend. We were both dealing with some issues. The speaker began to talk, and it seemed as if she was speaking directly to the both of us. She turned the lights on, and our issues began to run like roaches. My friend left. She told me that it was too hard to hear the truth. I remained, although I was uncomfortable. I often think about that event and that speaker. I am a better person today because I was willing to let the light come on and allow my issues to be exposed.

Issues 59

Issues left to simmer on the stove will one day boil over.

I can't imagine leaving a pot on the stove to simmer for twenty years. Are you placing your issues on the back burner instead of dealing with them? Avoiding them won't make them go away. Whatever they are, there is help and hope. Make the decision to take the issues off the stove and deal with them before they boil over.

Issues 60

If you announce that you have no issues, that is an issue.

If you act as if you are "issue free," that is an issue. It is impossible to be issue free.

If you are hiding the issues under the bed or in the closet, that is a problem. Don't allow your issues to define who you are by allowing them to hide. If you address them, you will become a better person.

Leadership 61

Have you hit the proverbial glass ceiling? A leader has to do what a leader has to do. It is time to use glass cutters and cut through the barriers.

My sixth-grade teacher, Mrs. Stokes, gave me my first glass cutter. She became one of the most important leaders in my life. She believed in me and planted seeds of confidence that I have never forgotten. We must understand the power of giving glass cutters to others. There will be many roadblocks, detours, potholes, and locked doors that will try to keep you from reaching or achieving your dreams. From the CEO of a company trying to hold it together to a single mom going back to school and raising four kids, many of us are striving to get ahead and carrying our glass cutters—so watch out!

Leadership 62

An exceptional leader doesn't run when adversity swarms around her head. She purchases a bigger fly swatter.

As a leader, you will be faced with adversity. Your strength lies in your ability to execute, lead, and produce results in the midst of the adversity. We must embrace who we are as women, and that may mean crying when no one is looking. The next time adversity swarms around your head, pick up your hot-pink flyswatter and start swatting the heck out of it.

Leadership 63

They say it's a man's world. However, women are their landladies.

Women are the glue that holds the world together. From the boardroom to the soccer field, we are there. We spend countless hours supporting, listening, encouraging, leading, fixing, managing, creating, and, oftentimes, mopping up the spills others have made. It would be an marvelous experience if, for one day, all the women in the world had a girls' night out. But then, who would run the world?

Leadership 64

Leaders don't jump into the lifeboat when the ship begins to sink. They fix the holes.

We are all leaders in some capacity. Your commitment as a leader is revealed during the company crisis or when not all is well at home. You may have to make a decision to stay on board and fix the holes—or jump overboard. The lifeboat may appear to be the easy way out, but think twice before you leap.

Leadership 65

How do you become a great leader? Begin each morning with a hot cup of humility.

I love to hear stories about the owners of companies who didn't take a salary but paid their staff instead, or the mother who knew her child had a special talent and paid for gymnastics lessons by taking a second mortgage on her home. These heroes had to humble themselves to ensure someone else would succeed. If we only practiced being humble, the world would be a better place. And in the end, by giving more of ourselves or not being the first in line, we end up with all that we need—and some leftover.

Life 66

My life is sometimes a hot, greasy, fishy mess.

Life is sometimes like frying fish. It can be very messy. Your teenager is not talking to you and has enough tattoos to open an art gallery, your marriage is on the rocks, and your job has you so stressed out that when you open your office door, the panic attacks begin. Life and all the grease can overwhelm you, but you must learn to function with the grease because you are not in preschool. Life doesn't give you time-outs.

Life 67

You have been sitting on the bench all of your life. It's the fourth quarter. It is time to get into the game before it's too late.

Think of your life as a basketball game. Some of us are in the first quarter; some, in the last. What matters is that you are playing. Don't allow yourself to be a bench warmer. Regardless of the quarter you are in, it is not too late. Make the decision to get in the game today.

Life 68

Treat life like a bottle of catsup. Squeeze all that you can out of it until there is nothing left.

I can't stand to waste anything. Because of this, I will get all of the contents out of a jar until there's nothing left. We should treat life in the same manner. We must learn to squeeze all that we can out of life. Think of it this way: some of us will die with a bottle still partly full, and some of us will die with an empty bottle. Is your bottle still full?

Life 69

Warning: enter at your own risk. My life is currently under construction.

Our lives are like construction sites. There will be renovations, remodeling, and even some demolitions. We are a work in progress. I have learned that life has various stages and phases. Just when I repair one area in my life, another needs to be fixed. If your life has never been under construction, you may be playing it too safe. Perhaps it is time for you to put your hardhat on and begin remodeling your life.

Life 70

Stop! Don't throw the broken pieces of your life away. You are a masterpiece.

Who knew the old painting in your neighbor's garage was worth millions? We have all heard those unbelievable stories. What is the lesson? How many times have we assumed an individual's self-worth based on how they looked? How often have we looked at our own self-worth based on our shortcomings instead of our potential, which is often hidden like the valuable painting found in the cold, damp basement of an abandoned house. You are a masterpiece. Don't underestimate your value.

Love 71

I remember our first date as if it were yesterday. Our love is still rich and sweet like my grandmother's peach cobbler. Over the years, we have had our battles, disappointments, and differences and have shed many tears. We are still laughing and still dancing. I want you to know that near or far, I will always love you.

Lasting love is much deeper than puppy love because it usually means that you have been together for a number of years, which means you have history together. Like a novel, you have many chapters to your relationship. They will be filled with excitement, disappointments, regrets, tears, good times, and bad times. The question is this: are you still dancing and laughing? How will the last chapter be written? Many relationships will never have a final chapter because they won't last. If you have managed to stay together, celebrate your accomplishments. If you are starting over, declare that you will dance this time.

Love 72

We were given many gifts on our wedding day. However, I don't recall getting the secret formula for a successful marriage. So we created our own: Commitment + Faith + Give and Take +Hard Work +Perseverance= A Successful Marriage.

Every marriage is unique and will require its own formula to be successful. The formula that works for one couple may not work for another. You and your partner will create your own formula based on those characteristics you have each identified as essential to making your marriage work.

Love 73

Make sure your sugar daddy is not made out of artificial sweetener.

My mother often says, "Everything that shines is not gold." The guy who picks you up for a date in the sports car is renting it, and the man you think is a stock boy is actually the owner of the company. The lesson is that looks can be deceiving, so don't be too quick to turn the stock boy down for a date.

Love 74

Love will require you to take risks. There are no refunds.

You take a risk when you love. It doesn't come with a warranty. Sometimes, you don't find out who you really fell in love with until the storms come. You thought he would stand by your side forever, but instead, he abandoned you. You thought that when you gained an extra twenty pounds after baby number three, he would still find you attractive. Try not to get swindled by love. Make your selections wisely, or you take the risk of going bankrupt.

Love 75

You must get a French manicure on your wedding day, but don't forget to pick up your hot-pink combat boots. Trust me—you are going to need them.

When I see newlyweds, I find myself thinking, "Are they prepared for war?" That may sound negative, but you will have battles. I am speaking from my own experiences from being married for almost thirty years. I am often asked, "What is the secret?" My response, with a laugh: "I keep my combat boots under my bed." Through adversity, you must be willing to fight for your marriage as a team and make a commitment like soldiers to never leave one another's side.

Self-Worth 76

If you are not willing to invest in yourself, then why should the bank?

Are you willing to take a risk on yourself? Too often, we wait for others to lend us money, confidence, self-esteem, and even love. Take the time today to conduct an appraisal of how valuable you really are then decide on an investment you will make in yourself.

Self-Worth 77

Never rely on others to conduct an appraisal of your self-worth.

Think of yourself as a treasure box filled with precious jewels. The jewels represent your abilities and talents, and they are sometimes not visible to others. When we rely on others to determine our value, we risk being devalued.

Self-Worth 78

There is one obstacle blocking you from being the best. It is you.

Is it possible that you are your own worst enemy—that you don't really believe in yourself? Is it your little secret? Are you a good actor, easily fooling everyone around you into believing you have it all together? You can sabotage your own success by not embracing yourself. You need to become your own best friend, your own most passionate advocate.

Self-Worth 79

Pretending is an excellent makeup concealer; it allows you to cover up the real you.

There are billions of people on the planet, but there is only one you. Challenge yourself. Take a look at who you really are without makeup and declare, "I am willing to be myself every day."

Self-Worth 80

You keep lip-synching your girlfriend's song because you are afraid to sing your own.

It takes some of us a lifetime to get the courage to sing our own song. I am constantly telling my daughter to be herself, and that there is no one else on the planet like her. If we learn in the beginning of our lives to stick to our own sheet of music, we won't waste time trying to look at someone else's. If you have not been singing your own song I challenge you to start today—before it is too late.

Success 81

Critics are like flies: they swarm around the picnic table when success is being served.

Like flies swarming around grilled hot dogs, baked beans, and potato salad during the picnic, some people may enjoy criticizing success. Learning how to accept constructive criticism from your critics can be turned into a positive experience. Gaining insight and information from others that was perhaps missed during the creative process can be used to secure and enrich your success.

Success 82

You can't microwave success. It has to be slow-cooked.

There is nothing more delicious than a slow-cooked roast. It seems to melt in your mouth. You cooked it slow and low. Success is often obtained in the same manner. It is a process that takes much time—sometimes years—depending on the venture. My advice is to get rid of the microwave and buy a crockpot.

Success 83

The road that leads to success often has the most potholes.

I began writing at the age of eleven. It seems as if I have been traveling on the road to success forever. I can't count the roadblocks, detours, breakdowns, and running out of gas that I have experienced. My advice is to buckle your seatbelt because the ride is bumpy on the road traveled to achieve success.

Success 84

To attend success's university, you must first attend failure's junior college.

In order to succeed, you must first fail. I have obtained a lot of knowledge from my failures. Your failures are your best teachers. One of my mentors told me, "Karen, you must be prepared to fail. You may fail ten times before you get it right." A big lump formed in my throat, and fear seemed to engulf the room. I knew then that I had to face my fears and accept failure as part of life. Some of the most successful people often have the most failures. The lesson? If you have failed, you are ready to attend success's university.

Success 85

Success will follow when diligence is the leader.

It takes diligence to obtain success. You must be willing to keep working, even when you don't see the immediate results. It is easy to start, but will you still have passion when you don't have any sales or when your idea is rejected ten times and the bank doesn't approve the loan? What do you do? You don't abandon your dreams; instead, you stick with them, and one day soon I guarantee you will see the fruits of your labors.

Tenacity 86

Tenacity is like glue. It sticks to its dreams until they become a reality.

I was often told by my parents growing up, "Karen, you must have bulldog tenacity if you want to succeed." There are thousands of good ideas, but how many of them will become a reality? Are you willing to stick with your dreams, or will you allow adversity to separate you from them?

Tenacity 87

Fly-by-night friends are easily detected. They don't have tenacity. They will drop you like a hot frying pan as soon as you need their support during the challenging times.

Commitment requires tenacity. You must be willing to go the distance, and you must have stamina. Unfortunately, this is a trait that is hard to find. Most people become weary and give up and move on to the next new thing or friend rather than sticking it out during the rough times.

Tenacity 88

Tenacity is like wearing a pair of boxing gloves. They provide support when fighting the doubters in your life.

If you have big dreams and aspire to do the almost impossible, you must be prepared to fight the doubters. Some people can put out the flames of greatness in your life quicker than the fire department. Remember: when your time comes, the doubters will see you as a contender who can't be beaten.

Tenacity 89

Tenacity can identify the weak players on the team. Like ice cream in a cone on a hot summer day, they begin to melt under pressure.

A team can only be successful if everyone on the team is willing to succeed when the air conditioner is not working and it's one hundred degrees. If you want to win at the game of life, you must be willing to play during high heat, hazardous conditions, and even during tornado warnings.

Tenacity 90

A relationship without tenacity is like a skyscraper built on sand and without a steel frame.

You won't find out what your relationships are made of until they are challenged. Once a storm is over, the sturdy buildings are still standing, and the poorly built ones are blown away like a doll's house. The spouse chooses to stay despite the extramarital affair. The coach signs on for another year because she sees the potential to win, despite no wins during the season. The parent never give up on their children, despite them still trying to find themselves in their mid-thirties. Time will reveal whether your relationships have been built on sand or concrete.

Thank You 91

Your generosity during my illness was a ray of sunshine during my hour of darkness. You didn't hesitate to respond. Thank you for carrying me when my knees were too weak to stand.

I found out what generosity meant when I was recovering from surgery. I was in a great deal of pain and very weak. Like special forces, my true friends came to my rescue with food, flowers, hugs, prayers, and a lot of, "Just let me know what you need." I was humbled and moved. I am still saying thank you, because during one of the darkest hours in my life, they provided me with sunlight and support.

Thank You 92

Our tears could fill a coffee cup. You have been a faithful friend. Thank you for allowing me to be myself. I don't have to pretend that I have it all together. You have seen me at my worst—without makeup, my hair not washed. I'm glad you are in my life.

I will never forget the women who changed my life. I became a member of a monthly women's group while living in Maryland in 2000. I was dealing with some major challenges, wounded and at times distraught. I entered their doors a broken woman, and for the first time in my life, I was able to be transparent. They helped to nurse me back to health with a lot of hugs, prayers, and words of hope. They demonstrated to me what sisterhood was all about. We should be sensitive to our girlfriends and their needs. Don't underestimate hugs or words of encouragement; they can make all the difference in a friend's life.

Thank You 93

I woke up this morning to watch the sun rise. I thought, ***What really matters in life? Not the number of designer shoes or handbags.*** **What matters are our friendships. Because the last time I had a crisis, the shoes and hand-bags didn't come over at two a.m. It was you. Thank you for being there.**

You spend a lifetime accumulating things, but take a moment and think about what really matters. Life doesn't warn you or tell you when you are going to need a friend. Your stuff can't provide comfort. Take inventory today of your life and friendships and keep only what you really need. Get rid of superficial things and focus on gratitude for your true friends.

Thank You 94

There are two words in the English language that can change the world—*thank you*.

I was raised old school. I was taught by parents to say thank you and to never take acts of kindness for granted. I have taught my kids to write thank-you notes and to say thank you. As a society, we have lost some of the old-school values. We shouldn't take it for granted when others go out of their way to help us or provide assistance. Showing gratitude more often can change the world and make so many people smile. The cost? It is free.

Thank You 95

What you say to others can inspire them to unleash the best that lies within them. "Thank you" is the key that unlocks the hearts of humankind.

When we appreciate the others in our life—from the mail carrier to the babysitter—we never run out of grace or acts of kindness. Don't wait until you find yourself at the mercy of others to acquire the spirit of gratitude. Practice saying *thank you*.

Winners 96

Winners are often found emptying the trash. They are not afraid to get their hands dirty.

Are you willing to get your hands dirty? Are you willing to do what others don't do? If you listen to the stories of successful people, they often got their hands dirty and had to walk in the mud to attain their dreams. We are deceived because we see the success and not the garbage they had to deal with before attaining it. The next time you see a successful woman, look at her shoes. They are covered in mud.

Winners 97

A winning team must be prepared to jump the hurdles of defeat.

It is impossible to create a winning team and never experience defeat or adversity. How do you prepare to win? The first step is to learn how to deal with defeat. It is not always the smartest, quickest, or most talented team that wins. It is the team that gets knocked down but gets back up that wins. The ability to win when defeat is staring you in the face is a quality that enables you to attain the championship rings in all areas of your life. Don't be too quick to run around defeat's hurdles. Instead, learn how to jump over them.

Winners 98

Winners treat disappointment like a badly cooked meal. They don't eat it.

Disappointment is like paying taxes: it is guaranteed to happen. None of us will be able to count the disappointments we will experience during our lifetime, but how we respond to them can make the difference. Winners choose to see the positive in every situation. Don't allow disappointment to give you heartburn. Remember, you don't have to eat it when it is served.

Winners 99

You can't jog to the finish line if you intend on winning. You must sprint.

I love watching women's track and field. Prior to the race, stories about the runners are often featured. This makes the race even more exciting because, as the viewer, you realize how hard they have worked and that they often had to overcome many difficult circumstances to become contenders. The gun is fired, and off they go. Like graceful stallions, they run toward their goals and dreams. But it is often the runner who sticks her chest out and sprints to the finish line who wins.

We must learn to stick our chests out and sprint—not jog—if we want to win.

Winners 100

Are you still swimming in the baby pool? Remember, winners are risk takers; they are willing to swim in the ocean to obtain their dreams.

Are you playing it safe—living in a comfort zone? In order to become a winner, you must be willing to take risks. Have you ever watched programs that feature information about the ocean? They explore the deepest parts of the ocean with their cameras to capture images of sea life and plants that would never be discovered in shallow waters. They often put their own lives at risk to pursue their dreams and passion. It is time to put the scuba diving equipment on and explore your deepest passions, girlfriend.

Conclusion

I hope you have been inspired to give your dreams their wings and go on the journey with me to discover your purpose in life. When you make the decision to embark on the journey, remember that you are not alone. Look into the sky and you will see millions of butterflies. They are resilient, determined, united, and flying—despite the holes in their wings.

12944348R00067

Made in the USA
San Bernardino, CA
05 July 2014